This is my book. My name is:

_____

LUCY THE EASTER CHICK

Copyright © 2023 by Victoria NaBozny Mayhugh
Cover design and illustrations by Jessica Lee

ISBN 978-1-7372160-8-7 (paperback)
ISBN 978-1-7372160-9-4 (eBook)

All rights reserved. No part of this book may be reproduced or transmitted in any form or by any means, electronic or mechanical or used in any manner without written permission of the copyright owner except for the use of quotations in a book review.

This is a work of fiction. Names, characters, places and incidents either are the product of the author's imagination or are used fictitiously.

A review of LUCY THE EASTER CHICK on Amazon
would be greatly appreciated.
Thank you!

Contact Victoria at
thetometime@gmail.com
for coloring art.

Laugh & Learn with Lucy! Happy Easter 2023! Victoria

LUCY THE EASTER CHICK

Written by Victoria NaBozny Mayhugh

Illustrated by Jessica Lee

In loving memory of my husband,
Wallace "Wally" Mayhugh
&
My wonderful parents,
Albert & Stella NaBozny
&
Dedicated to my lovable nieces & nephews,
Norman, Veronica, Griffin, Stella, Claudia & Eleanor
&
A special thank you to a special friend

It all started when Emma and her younger brother Bobby made Lucy their pet chick. They loved her because Lucy was a tiny bundle of soft feathers. She was different from her sisters and brothers.

Then one day, Lucy started laying eggs --- big, beautiful and very different eggs. They were pink and green, blue and yellow and orange and purple. Every night Lucy dreamed she was the Easter Chick, which made her happy.

Lucy told her Mommy and Daddy about her dream. They said there was only the Easter Bunny. But they smiled at Lucy and said, "Honey, some dreams come true."

So happy little Lucy kept busy laying eggs for Easter.
She was little, but her eggs were humongous.

Lucy strolled around the farm every day.
"Hi, I'm going to be the Easter Chick,"
Lucy clucked to her friends.
"Moo, moo! Good for you," Carrie Cow mooed.
Dudley Dog barked.
Connie Cat purred.
Tommy Turtle poked out his head.
Daisy Duck quacked.
Bella Birdy chirped congrats.
Stinky Skunk fluffed and shook his tail.
Peter Pig oinked. Benny Beaver slapped his tail.
"Baa, baa, baa," Godfrey Goat bleated
and chewed his cud.
Henry Horse whinnied.
Freddy Frog croaked.

Lucy saw her friend, Easter Bunny, hopping around the farm.
"Hi, I'm laying a lot of eggs for you. Maybe I could be the Easter Chick and help you deliver baskets to the children?"

"That is a great idea," Easter Bunny said.

They hugged. Then Lucy flapped her wings and hurried back to lay more eggs. Now Easter Bunny was sad. She had to do something to make Lucy the Easter Chick.

Lucy's Mommy and Daddy told Lucy it was time to deliver her eggs to the Easter Bunny. "I'm sad, Mommy and Daddy because I wanted to be the Easter Chick. But I will take all my eggs to the Easter Bunny."

"Lucy, your eggs will make the children happy this Easter," her Daddy said.

"I love you, Lucy, even though you are not the Easter Chick. You have a special gift. Your Father and I are very proud of you and your beautiful eggs."

Lucy sat atop her eggs for the last time. Now she had to deliver them to the Easter Bunny.

"Thank you, Lucy. Your beautiful eggs will make the children happy," Easter Bunny said. "I wished you could have helped me and been the Easter Chick." "That is okay," Lucy said, hugging her friend.

All Easter Bunny needed was permission from Sir Jack, a super-duper giant jackrabbit with eight-inch ears. He has been protecting the Great Cottontail Kingdom since Stinky Skunk rescued Sir Jack from a band of coyotes.

That night, guided by the light of the full moon, Easter Bunny hopped a mile to Sir Jack's grassland hideaway. Stinky Skunk, Dudley Dog, Connie Cat and Henry Horse joined Easter Bunny on the journey. Stinky Skunk would protect them from all enemies.

"Why have you come here so late?" Sir Jack asked.
He jumped six feet and frowned at Easter Bunny.

"I want to share my duties as the Easter Bunny with my friend Lucy. She magically lays big beautiful eggs," Easter Bunny said, showing Sir Jack a basket of Lucy's eggs.

Sir Jack was silent. He inspected Lucy's eggs. Then he jumped six feet and twitched his nose at Easter Bunny. "Wow! Your friend's eggs are special," Sir Jack said. "I proclaim that Lucy will be the Easter Chick."

"Thank you, Sir Jack," Easter Bunny smiled and flapped her ears. "You have made me and all of Lucy's friends happy." Easter Bunny was so happy she cried "tears of joy."

The next day Lucy was crowned the Easter Chick at a barnyard party. Everyone was happy.

"We will have fun together," Easter Bunny said, hugging Easter Chick.

Bobby jumped with joy, and Emma cried happy tears.

On Easter morning, Easter Bunny and Easter Chick surprised children with baskets filled with chocolate bunnies, chocolate chicks and Easter Chick's big, beautiful, colorful eggs.

And Easter Bunny and Easter Chick always said those three little words --- I love you --- to each other.

COLOR IT

COLOR IT

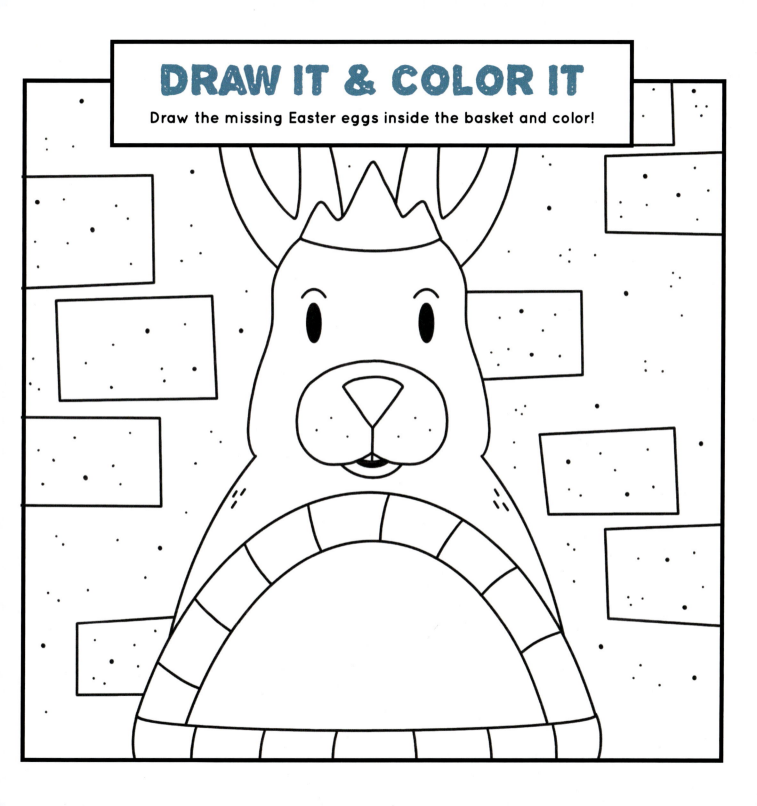

MATCH IT & DRAW IT

Draw lines to match the animal from LUCY THE EASTER CHICK with the sound it makes or what it does. You can peek back to the story for answers. Then draw a couple of animals.

LUCY	QUACKED
BELLA BIRDY	MOO, MOO!
TOMMY TURTLE	BAA, BAA, BAA
STINKY SKUNK	POKED OUT HIS HEAD
PETER PIG	CROAKED
CONNIE CAT	SLAPPED HIS TAIL
HENRY HORSE	CLUCKED
DUDLEY DOG	FLUFFED & SHOOK HIS TAIL
CARRIE COW	PURRED
GODFREY GOAT	OINKED
BENNY BEAVER	CHIRPED CONGRATS
DAISY DUCK	WHINNIED
FREDDY FROG	BARKED

LOOK IT UP

Victoria always challenges children to learn the meaning of new words. Here is a word list from LUCY THE EASTER CHICK.

BUNDLE .... A group of things tied together

COTTONTAILS .... American rabbits

CUD .... Food partially eaten then returned to the mouth to chew

DREAMED .... A series of thoughts during sleep

EASTER .... A Christian feast day celebrating the resurrection of Jesus

EASTER BUNNY .... A rabbit that brings baskets with candy & eggs to children

EGGS .... Hard-shelled food laid by certain animals

FARM .... Land for growing crops & raising animals

HIDEAWAY .... A secret place

HUMONGOUS .... Extremely large; huge

JACKRABBIT .... A rabbit with large ears & long hind legs

KINGDOM .... Land ruled by a king

MAGICALLY .... Special power

PERMISSION .... Approval

PROCLAIM .... To declare

STROLLED .... A slow & calm walk

TWITCHED .... A short, sudden jerking or movement

VICTORIA'S BOOKS

LUCY THE EASTER CHICK is Victoria's fourth book in her A 3 little words book series. Her other books are Mr. Mosquito Stay Out of My Pants, Mr. Wally and His Funny Little Hat and Chop! Chop! Mr. Christmas Tree! Her next book will be Lady and the Lonely Little Goose.

Contact Victoria at thetometime@gmail.com for coloring art.

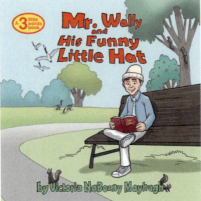
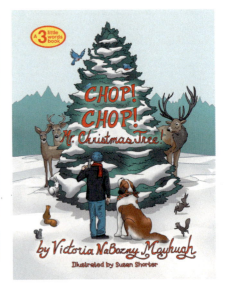
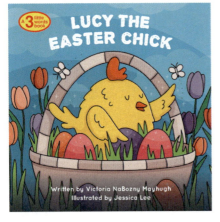
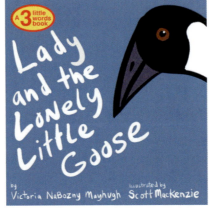

**THE AUTHOR
VICTORIA NABOZNY MAYHUGH**

VICTORIA NABOZNY MAYHUGH was born in Jackson, MI. She attended Ferris State University, graduated from Michigan State University with a degree in journalism and was a reporter/education writer and editor on newspapers in Iowa and Ohio.

LUCY THE EASTER CHICK is the fourth book in her A 3 little words book series. Her next children's book will be Lady and the Lonely Little Goose. Her first adult mystery, The Paste Pot Murders, will be published soon.

Based on the stories in her books, children are challenged to learn the meaning of new words, color pictures and draw their own creations.

Writing has been her passion since fourth grade when Sister Mary Mathilda at St. Stanislaus Kostka School told Victoria to post her story on the wall.

She lives in West Bloomfield, MI. Her loving husband, Wally, has been the inspiration for her books.

**THE ILLUSTRATOR
JESSICA ANN LEE**

JESSICA ANN LEE graduated from Eastern Michigan University with a BFA focusing in Graphic Design & Illustration. Outside of working as a graphic designer and freelance illustrator, she enjoys spending time outside, spoiling her cats, and taking trips up north.

View more of Jessica's illustration work by visiting @jl.illustrates on instagram.

COLOR IT

Made in the USA
Middletown, DE
20 March 2023